Old PRESTWICK

by

Ken Andrew

Prestwick's Auld Kirk is dedicated to St Nicholas and dates from about the twelfth century. It and the ruins at Kingcase on the south side of the town were possibly the earliest stone buildings in the area. This view across Kirk Street shows the approach to the Auld Kirk before the surrounding fields were taken over for housing. A mature horse chestnut tree now grows in the corner behind the wooden barred gate where there is a well-tended house and garden – cattle are unlikely to be seen anywhere in the area today. The white cottages have also been replaced by more modern housing. The present church of St Nicholas in the Main Street dates from the start of the twentieth century, by which time the Auld Kirk's graveyard was filling up, leading to the development of the cemetery on the east side of town at Glenburn.

Bruce's Well, Prestwick.

© Ken Andrew, 2000

First published in the United Kingdom, 2000,
by Stenlake Publishing Ltd.
01290 551122
www.stenlake.co.uk

ISBN 9781840331257

Printed by
Berforts, 17 Burgess Road, Hastings, TN35 4NR

THE PUBLISHERS REGRET THAT THEY CANNOT SUPPLY
COPIES OF ANY PICTURES FEATURED IN THIS BOOK.

FURTHER READING

The following books are a selection of those consulted by the author during his research, none of which are available from Stenlake Publishing.

Ronald W. Brash, *The Tramways of Ayr*, 1983.
Geological Survey of Scotland, *Economic Geology of the Ayrshire Coalfields Area 111*, 1930.
Rev. Kirkwood Hewat, *A Little Scottish World*, 1894.
Neil Johannessen, *Telephone Boxes*, 1994.
Rev. Luke McQuitty, *The Book of St Cuthbert's*, 1937.
Alan Robertson, *Lion Rampant and Winged*, 1986.
John Strawhorn, *The History of Prestwick*, 1994.
Ian Welsh, *Prestwick in the '40s*, 1992.

The publishers wish to thank Alex McGowan for providing the pictures on pages 1, 2, 4–17, 20–30, 31 (both), 32, 33 (both), and 34–42. The remaining photographs are by the author.

According to tradition, King Robert the Bruce suffered from a skin disease akin to leprosy and visited Kingcase at Prestwick to drink the healing water from this well. Steps lead down to the well where a shield bears a saltire between the dates 1274 and 1329 with the inscription, "Restored by the town council of Prestwick, 1912." The gate has been kept locked for a number of years to preserve the site and the hillock behind is better groomed today in front of encroaching houses. A plaque has been placed on the railings behind where the gentleman stands and states "Bruce's Well. Known to have been in existence since the thirteenth century serving the needs of the community attached to the Spittal and Lazar House nearby and adjacent to the Church of St Ninian. King Robert I of Scotland (the Bruce) benefited from the waters of the well and generously endowed the lazar house." A modern St Ninian's Church and hall, for the Episcopal community, have been built on the left, while scanty remains of a very old building are found to the right.

INTRODUCTION

In 1983 some of the inhabitants of Prestwick celebrated their town's millennium. These celebrations were low key and not all of the townspeople joined in as the evidence for Prestwick having existed for 1,000 years was somewhat controversial. Proof hinges on a charter of 1600 granted by King James VI and written in Latin. This refers to the town and burgh of Prestwick having been created by the progenitors of James VI "beyond the memory of Man by the period of six hundred and seventeen years." The issue at stake is whether it is the existence of the town that stretches back that far or just the progenitors of James VI. On the basis of this document alone, few historians would accept the former.

No-one can say with any certainty when Prestwick was created or why. It stands on sandy, low-lying land which was marshy in places. It has no commanding hilltop sites which might have attracted a chieftain or lord in need of a fort or castle. Its water-courses such as the Pow Burn are small and fairly insignificant so it did not develop as a bridge-point. Sea levels have risen and fallen over the ages without creating the deep water or sheltered haven for a harbour. But despite these lack of advantages the town did develop for some reason and is now recognised as the oldest burgh in the county of Ayr, although the evidence suggests that the present-day village of Monkton may be the oldest part of the parish, with a church being established on the rising ground north of Prestwick. The church at Prestwick may have come later, administered like that at Monkton, from Paisley Abbey. The ruinous shell of St Nicholas Church is considered to be Prestwick's oldest surviving building although a hospice at Kingcase at the south end of the parish could have been established around about the same time as it was associated with Robert the Bruce in the thirteenth century.

While the seaport of Ayr to the south expanded from the Middle Ages onwards, the parish of Prestwick and Monkton grew very slowly. The improving communication route between the south-west and Irvine would help these mainly weaving and agricultural communities but most of the locals were relatively unaffected by it.

Some people benefited by providing hostelries for the passing travellers, while tolls for the use of the road were extracted on the southern boundary at Prestwick Toll. The tollgate is long gone, but the name still survives. Authorities have devised subtler means of taxing us today and we cannot evade our taxes as was done in the past by taking to the shore road, where a more direct line to the north led along the edge of the sea.

Two salt-pan houses, which used local coal, survive at Maryborough where salt was extracted from sea water for curing and preserving food. There were a number of similar enterprises around the Scottish coast, but Prestwick has the most substantial relics of the industry in the two prominent houses standing above the sea which may have combined dwellings with downstairs workplaces.

A 110 tons schooner was built in 1846 in the same area, but one report states that the ship stranded immediately after being launched into the shallow water. Several ships carpenters are listed in the Census Returns from 1841 and 1851, but there are no records of other ships being built. While small boats could be manhandled into the sea for fishing, there was no future for large craft inshore between Ayr and Troon.

The arrival of the Glasgow-Ayr railway gave Prestwick its impetus for expansion, though things moved slowly at first. Prestwick Station opened in 1839 but did such little business that it was closed, reopened, and closed again before finally becoming established in 1846.

The growth of the town was rapid thereafter. The railway brought holidaymakers from the Central Belt, keen to enjoy the fresh air and sea-bathing. Boarding houses were developed to house them during their stay. Some visitors enjoyed their stay so much that they retired there, while others realised that they could live in Prestwick and still travel daily to work around Glasgow.

Up to twenty-five trains per day stopped at Prestwick from Glasgow St Enoch Station in the 1930s, and half day and even evening excursions were popular in the summer months, since the city was only an hour away. Today's timetable has up to forty trains a day from Glasgow Central Station and although Monkton lost its station in 1940, Prestwick gained a second station in 1994 to serve its expanding airport.

The sandy soil at Prestwick might not be very good for cultivating crops, but along with the untamed dune hillocks, it offered ideal terrain for playing the increasingly popular game of golf. Twenty-one years after the opening of the railway station, the first Open Golf Championship was played over the links of Prestwick Golf Club and by the end of the century the town had four courses.

Prestwick's reputation as a coastal resort was greatly enhanced by the opening of a fine new Bathing Lake in 1931. This was the largest swimming pool in Scotland and could cater for 1,200 bathers and 3,000 spectators. The unheated water might have seemed colder than the Firth of Clyde at times, but at least the bathers had high walls sheltering them from the prevailing wind. In good summers the area was a sun-trap and its turnstiles clicked round all day.

While the coastal water's temperature was lower than many would have liked, it was surprisingly high for the latitude of the town. This was due to the north-eastwards surge of the North Atlantic Drift separating from the Gulf Stream to bring relatively warm water and mild air to south-west Scotland. In consequence, Prestwick rarely experienced fogs. Early aviators, relying on basic equipment, soon learned to appreciate the clear skies along the Ayrshire coast and were landing their flimsy aircraft in fields at Monkton during the 1930s. With the onset of the Second World War Prestwick became a major training area for pilots and navigators and its airport quickly developed. A mistake in navigation brought a pilot from Newfoundland to Prestwick instead of Ireland in 1940 and a new transatlantic route was discovered.

With Prestwick remote from German attack, but within reach of transatlantic flights, it became the focus for the ferry route flying aircraft from America to supply at first the R.A.F. with aircraft and then U.S. forces after they joined the war. Up to 300 aircraft a day were landing in the busiest period and by 1945 37,000 wartime crossings of the Atlantic had been made. The airport's future on the international map was secured.

Trains and aircraft have played a large part in the history of Prestwick. In the 1950s and '60s the motor car was becoming the most popular form of transport. With rising

3

wages and more leisure time, many families aspired to having a car and the freedom to travel wherever and whenever they felt like it. The number of day trippers from the city increased, but their stay might have lasted only four or five hours. Fewer people were booking into hotels and boarding houses and day visitors tended to bring their own picnics and shun the local shops. As travel companies packaged cheap holidays abroad, new fleets of jet aircraft were being developed to bring foreign resorts within a few hours of travelling time.

The decline in popularity of resorts like Prestwick was not helped by indifferent summers, when cloud, rain and chilly winds were clearing the coast of all but dog-walkers. The town's cinemas closed and although it now has an ice rink, concerns over the health risk of pollution in the sea have frightened off the once-numerous bathers

and dented the aesthetic appeal of the firth. Today, the attractions of Prestwick are appreciated more by the elderly than by the young.

It is hard to see how the town can regain its appeal to holidaymakers in great numbers again, as any scheme to create a mini-Blackpool would be a costly failure. Perhaps the town should look more to its heritage and champion the marvellous story of its airport and its founders, who include David McIntyre and the Marquess of Clydesdale who made the first flights over Mount Everest in 1933. Local authorities tend to look over their shoulders to see what other areas are doing, but Prestwick's needs now are for men of vision able to follow their own paths.

Single storey cottages and shops at the Cross mix with two-storey developments and the steepled Freemen's Hall of 1844 in this quiet street scene from the horse and trap era. As shops pushed northwards, the little front garden in the centre had to go and the house behind it is now a cafe. Known at the time as the Golf Cafe, this became a favourite haunt of teenagers in the 1940s when Mr Tognarelli sold his wonderful ice cream from it to background music from a pianola. The house behind the mercat cross was soon to witness commercial redevelopment as well. There is a remarkable contrast between this spacious scene and its counterpart today, when not only do the streets witness a constant flow of traffic, but the pavements are cluttered with bollards, chains, and other bits of street furniture installed in a bid to create an image for the town.

Prestwick, Prestwick Cross & Town Hall.

An open-top tram stands outside the Freemen's Hall at the northern terminus of the Ayr Corporation Tramways system. The passengers milling around it would be risking their lives today at what has become a very busy crossroads. James Gibson's workshops behind the mercat cross have obliterated the cottage seen in the last picture.

MARKET CROSS, PRESTWICK.

The mercat cross is reputed to be one of Scotland's oldest and bears the date '1777' from a renovation. It has been moved about on a number of occasions. Here it sits outside the Freemen's Hall at the junction of Kirk Street, opposite Alexandra Avenue. Bryson's Garage had its principal base in the quieter Midton Road but expanded on to this more public site to face on to a major road. Today a forecourt filling station and motorist's shop have replaced the chimney-cornered building. The restaurant across the road is now a dwelling.

The open-top trams ran initially for four miles from Prestwick Cross to St Leonard's Church in Ayr with an extension a year later to Burns Monument at Alloway. The tramway ran from 1901 to 1932. Plans to extend the route northwards to Monkton were abandoned and this tram is seen approaching the most northern point on its journey. The doubled rails are merging into a single track where drivers changed ends of the trams and sides of the loops for the return journey. The high wall on the right was destroyed later to allow the public to enjoy Boydfield Gardens. The well-stocked shopping area on the left has since been infiltrated by travel agents, bookies and an art gallery reflecting the different priorities of today's citizens. The Cyclists Rest has long since ceased to be a viable enterprise as cycling amidst today's traffic in busy town centres has become a dangerous pastime.

Prestwick, Main Street.

The steeple and roof of the South Church date from 1884 but the houses and shops have changed greatly since this picture was taken at the junction of Main Street with Kyle Street and Gardiner Street, although the three-storey block still stands. The trams had a top speed of ten miles per hour so the little dog in the middle of the road was in no great danger. The area behind the cart has a much harder-edged look about it now, with box-like dormers and flat-roofed shops mainly taking the place of the pitched-roofed dwellings.

8

Prestwick Post Office stands beside the South Church in the handcart era. A chemist occupies the premises now with a hairdresser next door. The Central Bar is still there and, along with its close, is little changed. The post office moved to grander premises at the Cross in the 1920s, with a courtyard for vans outside the sorting office.

The tower of the North Church on the right, designed by John Keppie, was erected in 1896. Apart from the appearance of the garage and the shopfronts, the buildings are much the same as they are in this 1930s photograph. The clumsy looking buses had become efficient enough by 1932 to put the trams out of business, although the cables and rails were still to be lifted.

The Cross, Prestwick.

The central garden area in this picture gave access to underground toilets, opened in 1911. Due to its proximity to a bus stop the mercat cross was moved in 1963 to this island after the toilets were filled in. The high wall on the left was replaced by the red sandstone post office in 1928, while more recent redevelopment has closed off the road under the window shades, and traffic lights control the redesigned junction. It was in the Red Lion on the right that the Prestwick Golf Club was formed in 1851.

Behind its crescent of sandy shore, Prestwick's dunes still awaited taming by the time of this 1897 photograph. Farther inland, the line of two-storey villas had laid down a frontier for the town, and the battle to control the dunes was soon pushing grass turf and concrete walls westwards to hold back the sand.

The seaside offered brief periods of freedom to the Victorians and Edwardians, allowing them to escape from long hours of work and to partly cast off the constraints of fashion and decorum. In this 1902 photograph entertainers hold an overdressed audience's attention among the dunes at the foot of Grangemuir Road. Ponies, boats for hire, and entertainment on makeshift stages are out of fashion today. The landscape was soon 'municipalised' – the dunes were removed and a seawall and lamp-lit promenade laid down, backed by plots of grass and a toilet block. More recently, a car park and flanking access road were also installed. The nearest house on the right was long sought after by developers for the spacious grounds it sat in and their persistence has been rewarded – the two-storey house has vanished and Ailsa Craig View, a four storey complex of retirement flats, now looks out to the firth.

13

By 1909 an esplanade had conquered the dunes and permanent facilities had been constructed for visitors and beach entertainers. Not too permanent, however, as the flagpoled kiosk, toilets, and beach pavilion are unrecognisable today in the redeveloped site occupied by a health and fitness club and Prestwick Sailing Club. Above the pavilion is the roof of St Nicholas Golf Club before additions were added to it. The grass on the left has long since been cleared for the car park.

14

The Smart Set Cadets were a popular troupe offering a summer season of entertainment on the seafront in Edwardian days. In this 1911 photograph they are performing the 'Sunshade Song'.

What a difference a century makes. Liberated sun-worshippers have little time for clothes or restraints on our beaches today, but in the early 1900s convention demanded the utmost modesty. The ladies wore high collars and ankle-length skirts while the men sweltered in suits. Bathing machines stand by the sea so that bathers could dash quickly from them into the water before anybody could see their bare arms and legs. On the day this photograph was taken, however, the choppy looking water indicates that the wind may have helped people to keep their clothes on.

Prestwick from St. Nicholas Tower, looking N.E.

This view from the belfry of the St Nicholas Church steeple looks along Main Street and round the bend towards the South Church. The photograph was taken before the steeple's dominance as a landmark was challenged by developments north and south of the town centre. The Royal Hotel with its garage, lock-ups and petrol pumps has been replaced by the Butlers House Hotel. Above and to the left of the site can be seen the Picture House, opened in 1913 and demolished in 1973.

Redevelopment at Prestwick Toll in 1968, looking from Pleasantfield Road towards the shops on Ayr Road. The new five-storey block on the right was one of four, all named after Scottish and Irish islands. The huts and space beyond were about to be replaced by a car park and a new Toll Bar, while the boarded-up block with the outside stairs would be replaced by a single storey row of sheltered housing.

18

Seaton's Garage and the two-storey house to its left have now been replaced by a flat-roofed Safeway supermarket and car park at Prestwick Toll. Farther along the same side, the sports pavilion (used by golfers and later by football teams) and the house in the middle distance were removed to make way for the Centrum Arena, a huge ice rink opened in 1996. The Toll Bar on the left has found new premises behind the position from which the picture was taken, while the former site along with the two-storey sandstone tenement in the foreground has been redeveloped for sheltered housing. The Belisha Beacon crossing was an infamous accident area, marginally improved when the 'keep left' islands were installed. Pedestrian-controlled traffic lights have greatly helped, but with two new turn-offs in quick succession to the supermarket and the Centrum, drivers need to stay very alert.

19

MUNICIPAL GOLF CLUB HOUSE, PRESTWICK.

This view at Kingcase from Ayr Road shows the start of St Ninian's Golf Course stretching to the east. By the 1950s the town was expanding to the south and east and parts of the course were developed for housing. A football pitch was marked out beside the pavilion and gardens were created in the foreground. More housing, a primary school, and the Centrum Arena and car park have left little space for the grass now.

170.

PRESTWICK GOLF COURSE.

The first tee at the Prestwick Golf Club. It was here in 1860 that Willie Park won the first Open Championship. The first twelve Opens were held here until St Andrews, Musselburgh and Muirfield joined in. A cairn now stands to the right of the flagpole commemorating that first ever championship, while shore-front flats fill in the skyline beyond it.

The Ladies St Nicholas Golf Club was established in 1893. The clubhouse shown here in this 1905 photograph stood east of the Ayr Road on ground that is now occupied by the indoor bowling club and the indoor swimming pool. The loss of the ladies course was mourned by many as it was enjoyed for its short holes and the relaxed atmosphere that prevailed. As a sign of the times, the flagpole has now been replaced by a fifty feet high mobile phone transmitter.

The Ex-Servicemen's Tennis Clubhouse sat between Templerigg Street and Mansewell Road. This was one of two sites in the town where the public could play tennis in the early 1930s. During the Second World War the building was converted and opened in 1943 as the 2001st 'British Restaurant'. These supplied war-workers, as well as the general public, with cheap, wholesome meals at a time of food shortages and rationing. The Prestwick restaurant functioned six days a week, increasing to seven in 1944. After the war the building became a youth club. Tennis was still available to the general public until the entire site was redeveloped for housing and new tennis courts were opened in 1954 at St Ninian's Park, the former ladies' golf course.

Tennis Court Prestwick

Along with the Mansewell Road courts, a second set of tennis courts (pictured) was listed in the 1934 town guide at St Ninian's Road. This site along with the South Beach Pavilion and kiosk in the background was soon to be redeveloped. The site of the tennis courts is now taken by a distinctive block of white-walled houses with five sets of double gables and steeply pitched roofs hung with red tiles. The terrace bends round the road junction and blocks off this vista to the shore.

The Putting Green, Prestwick.

Like many seaside resorts, Prestwick relied on its sandy shore and safe bathing to attract holidaymakers during the summer months. Behind the promenade, the putting green offered gentle exercise and amusement as a complimentary attraction. The well-clad putters suggest that the sea may have been a bit too chilly on this occasion.

Sea Bathing Lake, Prestwick.

The Bathing Lake was opened in 1931 at a cost of £37,000 and was the largest swimming pool in Scotland at that time. Of Olympic standards, it measured one hundred yards long and held one million gallons of water. It was a popular, well-patronised place for a number of years, but by the late 1960s indifferent summers and the unheated water were attracting only the hardy enthusiasts.

This later picture from 1933 shows the north dome with the gents changing rooms underneath, a floating platform, chutes and high diving boards all now in place. While the water could be cold and the wind very chilly, the high walls could make the place a sun-trap on a summer's day. The spectators' benches are much busier than the water, so the temperature may have been struggling to rise and no doubt the pipe band were quite happy to be wrapped up in yards of tartan. The deepest part of the pool lay under the high diving boards while the shallowest part was in the foreground where spectating parents could keep an eye on their children. The two domes of the Bathing Lake were very distinctive landmarks on the coastline, but they were demolished about a decade after their closure in 1972, along with the columned spectating area, changing rooms and the frontage of the building. The sea wall and the curved amphitheatre survive as its reinforced concrete construction would have made it very difficult and costly to remove. Instead, the local authorities made use of the site by turning it into a children's playground.

THE CHUTE, SEA BATHING LAKE, PRESTWICK.

Youngsters posing for the camera at the shallower end of the Bathing Lake. Some of the spectators seem overdressed for a summer day, and at least one pessimist is carrying a raincoat. An annual Bathing Beauty Contest was introduced in 1948 and gave the ladies the chance to show themselves off before crowds of 3,000 spectators or more.

Pavilion and Beach, Prestwick

The sun is out and the tide is in. As well as serving as a tearoom, the north kiosk could offer shelter to those caught out by a shower or to anyone wishing to get out of the sun or wind. The penny-in-the-slot weighing machine was once a very common piece of outdoor furniture, but is now rarely seen. The telephone box appears to be the modified K1 type which was introduced in 1927.

A view from 1938 when the Second World War was looming ahead and habits were changing. By that time, the car park was starting to fill up with cars, making it worthwhile for the council to employ an attendant to collect charges at the entrance box. After the war, greater mobility, higher wages, more free time and wider aspirations resulted in a gradual decline in Prestwick's appeal as a holiday resort. The closure of the kiosk and demolition of the Bathing Lake would follow. By this time the resited telephone box was a K6 Jubilee type introduced to the country in 1936. The meteorological station on the left was established in 1932 and readings from it were wired to the London met office daily. A large indoor leisure centre for children now sits to the right of the Bathing Lake site, while the horizon is dominated by the Ailsa Shipyard shed and Marine Highland Hotel at Troon.

THE GARDENS AND BATHING LAKE, PRESTWICK.

A.7575

If people were lackadaisical about going to church then the church went out to them, and where better to find an audience than on the seafront at the weekend. The missionary on his platform is holding his arms aloft to captivate his audience, but he seems to have lost the attention already of some of the younger folk in the front row.

Now that the minister has finished his sermon, the kids can get on with a wrestling competition in the sand.

NORTH BEACH, PRESTWICK.

554

At one time there was a keen demand for this line of chalets north of the Bathing Lake under the sand hills. Many families hired chalets for the summer season. Adults could relax in the doorways while keeping a watchful eye on their children enjoying the gently sloping beach and safe rippling waves.

In the official town guide for 1934 the Parkstone Hotel advert mentions "a dainty tearoom for non-residents". In the past hotel guests humped their luggage from the railway station or the bus route, or arrived by taxi. Nowadays they usually arrive by car and may stay for only a few hours in the restaurant or bar. This view of the hotel from Ardayre Road shows it having a garden area which has since been sacrificed for precious car parking space. The gable-ended section is still recognisable today but the gap on its left has been filled in to incorporate an extension, while the buildings right of the entrance have been subsumed in a curved two-storey function suite.

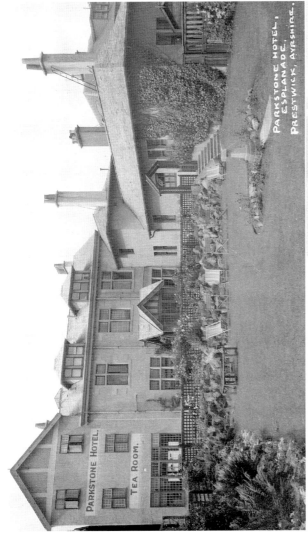

PARKSTONE HOTEL, ESPLANADE, PRESTWICK, AYRSHIRE.

PARKSTONE HOTEL.

TEA ROOM.

The Biggart Hospital and Home for Crippled Children was established in open countryside in the early years of the twentieth century with funds provided by Alexander Love Biggart, the Glasgow ship-owner and insurance broker. Prestwick's housing developments have since expanded to join it on the edge of town and extensions have greatly added to its size on the north and east sides. The wings have advanced forward of the central two-storey block with the three bowed windows, partly obscuring the distant wing running out at right angles. Some of the seats where patients could enjoy the fresh air have been removed to make way for a staff car park and the hospital now cares for geriatric and some younger patients.

The Miller's Dam, Prestwick.

A. McEwan, Prestwick.

RELIABLE SERIES

The Mill Dam on the Pow Burn looking towards Orangefield on the boundary between Prestwick and Monkton. The mill was a corn-mill but little of it remains today and the burn flows past the site with no restraints to form a pond. The area has been steadily eroded of its woodlands, by the airport on the right of the burn and by new housing on the left. The Pow is the largest of the small streams that meandered through the parish. When a golf course existed slightly downstream from the dam, the banks of the burn were worked assiduously by youngsters looking for lost golf balls in the water.

Mansewell Road, Prestwick

The houses are facing on to Mansewell Road which was actually just a pedestrian lane. What some claimed to be common land (now built on) separates it from the sidings of Prestwick Station (now renamed Prestwick Town Station to distinguish it from the one at Prestwick Airport). The view from the footbridge at the station looks over an assortment of mineral wagons, a covered van and horse and cart which play no part here now, as the sidings are no more and goods traffic moves in new ways.

Orangefield House gets its name from its one-time owner James Macrae's admiration for King William of Orange. Macrae had left his native Ayrshire to work in India near the end of the seventeenth century and had done so well for himself that he retired as Governor of Madras with a large fortune. Back in Ayrshire, he purchased Monkton House around 1736, rebuilt it, and nailed his colours to the mast as it were by renaming it Orangefield. One of the house's later owners was James Dalrymple, a friend and patron of Robert Burns. During the twentieth century the mansion became a hotel and then the hub of the airport.

A. 8866.

AERODROME, PRESTWICK.

A photograph from 1939 showing two-seater open cockpit Tiger Moths in front of their hanger. This was the early days at Prestwick Airport, when the centre of operations was found on the Monkton side of the main runway (there was little on the Prestwick side at that time). The airport was a training centre at that point for airmen who were soon to be flying with the Royal Air Force, but a fire in the administration block (in the background) in 1941 was an unfortunate setback to flying training.

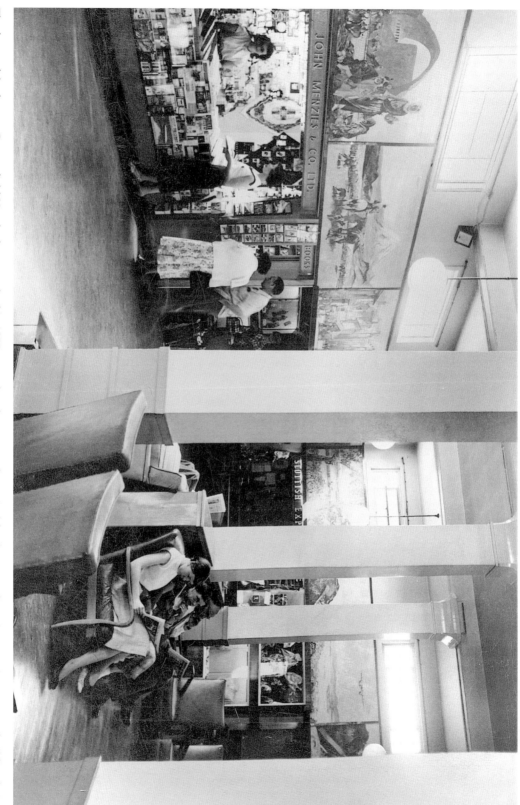

The foyer of the former Orangefield Hotel, photographed in 1955, served as the cramped terminal for the expanding airport prior to a new building being opened in 1964. Murals depicting scenes from distant lands encouraged thoughts of international travel and foreign trade.

SCOTTISH AIR LINES LIBERATOR AT PRESTWICK AIRPORT.

B.5.

Scottish Airlines was set up by Scottish Aviation at the end of the Second World War with hopes of opening up routes to Europe and North America as well as those on the domestic scene. However, nationalisation of the airways in 1946 ended the chance. The company's Liberator is seen in front of Orangefield which became the airport's headquarters in the 1940s. The control tower is far from elegant sitting among the chimney pots, but at least it gave the controllers a very good view of the runways.

Spectators at Orangefield in 1953 enjoying a close view of a Scottish Airline's Dakota. Scottish Airlines was set up in 1946 by David McIntyre, a local pioneer who with the Marquess of Clydesdale (his flying partner over Mount Everest in 1933) had previously established Scottish Aviation in 1935. Aircraft such as Dakotas and Liberators were war surplus planes adapted for passenger travel. The former control tower, offices and hangars of the early flying school can be seen across the main runway, along with a parking lot of U.S. bombers.

A SCOTTISH WELCOME, PRESTWICK AIRPORT.

Pipers giving a Scottish welcome to international travellers arriving at the airport. Numerous servicemen and women, dignitaries and others received their first, and possibly only experience of Scotland, on a refuelling stop at Prestwick. During the war, for security reasons, a distinguished list of famous people passed through without publicity including royalty, prime ministers, generals, admirals, atomic scientists and entertainers.

Golfers on the former St Cuthbert's Golf Course drive off below Redbrae. This was a huge red-roofed mansion which became a hive of activity during the Second World War when it was taken over by the airport to become the air traffic control centre. The house was demolished after air traffic control moved to Atlantic House at Glenburn in 1972 and the site is now a car park.

As the airport expanded, the main runway was lengthened to accept larger and more powerful aircraft. The Monkton to Prestwick road lay in the way so it was diverted farther and farther to the west in a loop. In this view from Monkton's Station Road the traffic is held up on the north side of the runway as an aircraft takes off above the road. Airport police controlled the crossing seven days a week from the white cabin in the centre. The rooftop control tower of Orangefield on the right gave a grandstand view of all take-offs and landings. Beyond the airport can be seen the Shaw Tower, an eighteenth or nineteenth century folly. To the right of it is Glenburn Colliery, while on its left is Mossblown Colliery bing, both of which were both in use at the time. The colliery and Orangefield have vanished from the scene. The bing is landscaped and the control tower has been replaced by vast cargo and servicing sheds.

An impatient motorcyclist evades the stop barrier ahead of clearance as traffic is held up for a landing U.S. seaplane. Waiting traffic can also be seen under the aircraft on the Prestwick side beside houses which have now been demolished. When a plane was due to land or take off, a warning bell sounded before the traffic lights turned to red and barriers were swung across the road. If you were walking across the end of the runway at the time you were encouraged to speed up. The journey between Monkton and Prestwick became a mile longer in the 1960s due to the diversion of this road to the west. The original route is unlikely to open again as giant cargo sheds now straddle the way.

A base for airmen from the U.S.A. developed along Monkton's Tarbolton Road from the days of the Second World War and through the succeeding years of the Cold War with the U.S.S.R. The relaxed dress code of the 'yanks' seen leaving the Greensite Base on the north side of the airport was envied by the much more regimented Royal Air Force. H.M.S. *Gannet*, a Royal Naval Air Station, took over the base from the U.S. in 1970. Security is much stricter, with barriers at the gate and high razor wire fences. The Search and Rescue helicopters based here have played vital roles in humanitarian missions such as mountain rescues and transferring sea casualties to hospitals.

The clubhouse of St Cuthbert's Golf Club looks down on an unplayable course which suffered periodically from the Pow Burn overflowing its banks after heavy rain. Half of the course could suffer in this way, but the temporary ponds were also liable to freeze in the winter and were enjoyed by youngsters skating or playing ice hockey. The club moved to the east side of Prestwick in the 1960s when a new terminal building was constructed for the airport to the right of the photograph, served by a new road which looks down on the Glenburn railway line and a housing estate from a higher causeway. The course of the railway line is almost lost now in the whin bushes, while a pumping station of West of Scotland Water occupies the far end of the fairways to the left and rises nearly as high as the old clubhouse still standing on the hill.

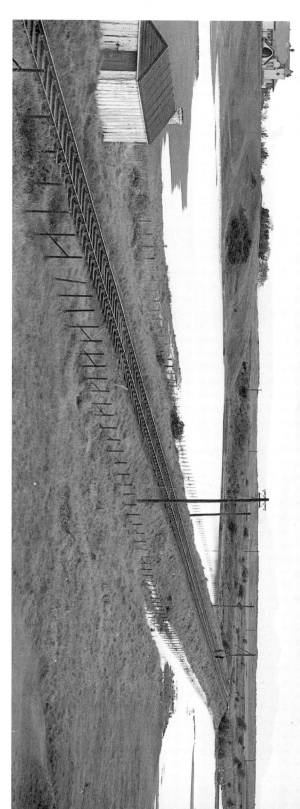

A colliery began production in 1912 at Glenburn on the east side of Prestwick. Auchincruive 4/5 as it was known officially (to distinguish it from its near neighbour at Mossblown, Auchincruive 1/2/3) employed up to 700 men at its peak before closing in 1973. Here the men on the day-shift return to the surface and head for the baths.

The northernmost of the three Glenburn rows looked down on the mineral railway line heading for Glenburn Colliery. The waste bing of Mossblown Colliery, also served by this line, can be seen in the distance. The railway carried on beyond Mossblown to Annbank Junction where it linked with other central Ayrshire lines, giving the system a flexibility that has been curtailed greatly since. The closure of all the collieries has been accompanied by a drastic rationalisation of the railways, leaving a much leaner network today.